BECAUSE YOU ARE WITH ME

BECAUSE YOU ARE WITH ME

Hope for the Journey from Psalm 23

By
A. D. Westbrook

RESOURCE *Publications* · Eugene, Oregon

BECAUSE YOU ARE WITH ME
Hope for the Journey from Psalm 23

Copyright © 2020 A. D. Westbrook. All rights reserved. Except for brief quotations in critical publications or reviews, no part of this book may be reproduced in any manner without prior written permission from the publisher. Write: Permissions, Wipf and Stock Publishers, 199 W. 8th Ave., Suite 3, Eugene, OR 97401.

Resource Publications
An Imprint of Wipf and Stock Publishers
199 W. 8th Ave., Suite 3
Eugene, OR 97401

www.wipfandstock.com

PAPERBACK ISBN: 978-1-7252-6485-4
HARDCOVER ISBN: 978-1-7252-6486-1
EBOOK ISBN: 978-1-7252-6487-8

Manufactured in the U.S.A.   JUNE 17, 2020

Scripture quotations taken from the New American Standard Bible® (NASB), copyright © 1960, 1962, 1963, 1968, 1971, 1972, 1973, 1975, 1977, 1995 by The Lockman Foundation. Used by permission. www.Lockman.org

Additional use of Scripture in chapter titles reflects the author's translation of the Hebrew text.

In loving memory of Sheri Benvenuti
We'll meet you down the road, my friend!
Ecclesiastes 4:12

CONTENTS

Preface | ix
Introduction | xiii

CHAPTER 1
Because You Are with Me:
I AM SECURE | 1

*The LORD is my Shepherd, I will not lack . . .
I will dwell in the household of the LORD forever.*

CHAPTER 2
Because You Are with Me:
I AM ENRICHED | 7

*In pastures of new grass He makes me stretch out and lie down . . .
Surely goodness and steadfast love will pursue me
all the days of my life.*

CHAPTER 3
Because You Are with Me:
I AM REFRESHED | 13

*To waters of quiet rest He tenderly guides me . . .
My cup is filled to overflowing.*

CHAPTER 4
Because You Are with Me:
I AM WHOLE | 19

He restores my soul . . . You heal my head with oil.

CHAPTER 5
Because You Are with Me:
I AM CONFIDENT | 25

*He leads me in paths of rightness because of His name . . .
You set before me a table facing my enemies.*

CHAPTER 6
Because You Are with Me:
I AM COURAGEOUS | 31

*Even if I walk in the darkest valley, I will not be afraid of harm . . .
Your rod and Your staff, they comfort me.*

Epilogue | 39

PREFACE

Several years ago, I was drawn to Psalm 23 in preparation for speaking at a retreat. I had studied Hebrew poetry and taught related courses over the years, but I had not specifically considered this well-known psalm from the perspective of its poetic form. It was a rich study and seemed to present an opportunity for devotional writing.

Little did I know what life was about to bring. I had shared a home with my two dear friends, Sheri and Sandy, for many years—we had become family. And then Sheri was diagnosed with pancreatic cancer. For a year and a half, we walked closely together through "the valley of the shadow," contending for healing and striving to trust the Lord for daily grace.

Several months into her treatment, my heart turned again to Psalm 23. I began to write, taking a few pages at a time to share with her. I also asked for her help to keep this book on hope-filled trust in the Lord well grounded in the realities of the hardships we sometimes endure. Real faith flourishes in real life—it is not an avoidance game.

Preface

As time went by, the Lord met us in that room, while we reflected together on the richness of His Word. I could see her being visibly sustained by His faithfulness, even as her body was failing. At one point, I suggested that perhaps the Lord had led me to the whole study just for the season we were walking through together. She was having none of that! Even in this most challenging time, Sheri continued to be concerned with others, as was her way. She insisted that the book be finished and published because other people would need this encouragement.

A few weeks later, we were with Sheri when the Lord received her from this life into the next. We rejoiced for our sister in her complete restoration—and we also began the long and arduous journey of unbearable grief in our own loss. The first year, reading the draft of this book was too painful because of precious memories of those last days with my dear friend. The second year, I faced significant health battles of my own, and came back to the manuscript in a time of despair, finding comfort and strength in the Word (the irony of Sheri's exhortation rang in my ears!).

In the third year, with improved health, I returned to the work of completing this book. As I began, we learned my mom had advanced cancer. Two months later, my dad died suddenly of a heart attack. And so, we grieve that loss and continue to walk with Mom through this part of her journey, while completing the final draft of this work for publication.

My own experiences of soul pain and physical challenges have both tempered and expanded my understanding of the Lord's promises and hope-filled encouragement in Psalm 23. He is continually faithful, and we continually learn the reality of total dependence on daily grace. It is a dependence that is a very good thing—because He is with us!

INTRODUCTION

Psalm 23 is perhaps the most well-known and treasured psalm in Scripture. People knowing little about the Bible are often familiar with these beautiful and comforting words from ancient times. Its peaceful pastoral scenes, given in stark contrast to the very real human fears of facing hunger, hostile enemies, and even death, cause its message to be both genuine and timeless, regardless of who you are or where and when you live.

The words alone are rich with promise and hope, but we might miss another important aspect of this beloved biblical text. This psalm, like all others, is really a poem. Consequently, not only do its individual words have meaning, the way they are arranged together also has meaning.

This aspect of the psalm may go unnoticed by those of us who are used to reading with linear thought—that is, moving simply from one point to the next, as if each thought were the next link in a straight chain.

In Hebrew poetry, there are also other ways in which the poet might arrange the ideas, and one of them seems to be the case with the poem we know as Psalm 23. This configuration, called a "chiastic" pattern, works something like a mirror. Each idea in the first half of the psalm has a reflective partner in the second half that restates it, contrasts it, or further explains it in some way.

In this format, the first line of the poem has a reflective partner in the last line of the poem. Then the second line in the poem parallels the second to the last line, the third line parallels the third from the last, and so forth until the two halves of the psalm meet in the middle. That middle point is the main point anchoring the entire poem.

Recognition of this pattern in Psalm 23 opens great opportunity for further understanding and reflection on what this poem communicates to the reader. Suddenly the placement of each idea in the psalm provides a reflective partner for us to consider as we think about its meaning. We might chart this out with lines showing the parallel ideas as follows:

```
The LORD is my shepherd, I shall not want.
    He makes me lie down in green pastures;
        He leads me beside quiet waters.
            He restores my soul;
                He guides me in the paths of righteousness for His name's sake.
                    Even though I walk through the valley of the shadow of death, I fear no evil,
                        For You are with me;
                    Your rod and Your staff, they comfort me.
                You prepare a table before me in the presence of my enemies;
            You have anointed my head with oil;
        My cup overflows.
    Surely goodness and lovingkindness will follow me all the days of my life,
And I will dwell in the house of the LORD forever.
```

By recognizing this intentional pattern in the psalm, we may explore the following pairing of ideas within it:

- The LORD is my shepherd, I shall not want . . . I will dwell in the house of the LORD forever

Introduction

- He makes me lie down in green pastures . . . Surely goodness and lovingkindness will follow me all the days of my life
- He leads me beside quiet waters . . . My cup overflows
- He restores my soul . . . You have anointed my head with oil
- He guides me in the paths of righteousness for His name's sake . . . You prepare a table before me in the presence of my enemies
- Even though I walk through the valley of the shadow of death, I fear no evil . . . Your rod and Your staff, they comfort me

As each of these combinations are considered together, we are led by the psalmist to the crescendo of the poem, the statement declared boldly at its center. Here, the psalmist celebrates the constancy of the LORD's presence as He relates to His people. Every other statement in the psalm centers on this truth, "Because You are with me."

With all these things in mind, this book is devoted to an exploration of the meaning of Psalm 23 with understanding of its poetic content. Each pair of reflective partners in the psalm will be considered, as well as their direct connections to the central point of this poem. The fact that the LORD is with me has tremendous impact on how I walk this journey of human experience with all its challenges and joys in a very real broken world.

Somewhat ironically, in modern times this psalm has become strongly associated with—perhaps even limited to—what we should read when someone approaches death. While Psalm 23 is a great comfort for such times, this psalm is really focused on how we experience the whole of life. And no matter what else it may hold, that is a journey worth taking—because He is with me!

CHAPTER 1

Because You Are with Me
I AM SECURE

The LORD is my Shepherd, I will not lack . . .
I will dwell in the household of the LORD forever.

What does it mean for the LORD to be with me? Psalm 23 explores the idea with much detail, as the writer reflects on the faithful presence of God in the lives of His people. At the center of this reflection lies a most profound truth—

Whatever else may be happening in my life at any given time, *the LORD is with me*.

Whatever else may be happening in my life at any given time, *I am not alone*.

This factor impacts every other circumstance that I encounter along the way, whether it be a glorious blessing or an experience more difficult than I ever thought I could endure.

The initial picture the psalmist provides for the reader to ponder along with this idea is that of the Shepherd. This imagery invites us to think of one who leads the flock into places of provision and safety. He guides the sheep, giving ongoing care and tending to the individual needs of each one in His charge.

Each sheep matters to Him—

I matter to Him—

It is personal.

This Shepherd is so utterly faithful in His ways that the sheep is assured of being free from lacking. It is important for us to recognize that the wording here for "lacking" does not actually focus on the person's act of needing, but rather upon the person's condition of having been made less.

In other words, the psalmist is not saying, "The LORD is my Shepherd, so I'll never experience loss," or "The LORD is my Shepherd, so I'll never go through difficult times." On the contrary, this psalm assumes that every life will include some very dark valleys to be crossed. But the vital truth here is that no matter what loss or gain I experience in this life, my identity, my worth, my true self will not be diminished.

This is about our state of being, not just a specific experience in the immediate circumstance. This is about abundant life—the wealth of personhood—the rich substance of my soul—regardless of what the day brings or the feelings that come with it. Whatever comes, the reality of my being will not be reduced. I will not be made less.

I Am Secure

This wealth of my secure condition is caused by the reality that the LORD is not just a Shepherd, but He is One who is shepherding. That is, the Shepherd is not identified simply as One with a title or a job description, but as One who is engaged in an ongoing and personal activity. The LORD is involved continually in the active work of tending to the rich and complete life and health of the sheep—the LORD is perpetually shepherding.

And, He is continually, actively shepherding *me*.

The LORD is constantly involved in the process of providing for me as one who is rightfully in His care. Whatever I might encounter along the journey, the depth of my being is not diminished because He is perpetually tending me—because He is with me.

How is this accomplished? The imagery of the Shepherd addresses practical concerns, which theoretically could be achieved in a distant sort of way. For example, the LORD, as Shepherd, could make sure the sheep gets food and water, while focusing the entire time on the fact the He, Himself, is not a sheep and that there is a great difference between His own identity as the Shepherd and the lowly place of the animal He tends.

The poetry here, however, denies this possibility in the picture of the LORD as Shepherd of His people. Instead, the parallel is drawn between the imagery of the Shepherd, who continuously provides for His sheep so that they will be complete, and the imagery of the family as a life-giving community. "I will dwell in the house of the LORD forever."

According to the psalmist, as part of the LORD's "flock," I am not only given basic provisions and care, but I am actually a member of the LORD's household.

Because You Are with Me

I belong—

    I have status—

        I have a name.

I have these things because I have been established for the long-term within the family of the living God. Because He is with me, I am entirely secure. He shares Himself with me. Because His identity is secure, I have a secure identity. I am part of a secure community, of which the Creator and Sustainer of all life is the Center.

This truth presses us toward a deeper understanding of what it means for the LORD to be "with me." There is a direct connection between the reality of who I am and my relationship with the LORD, who provides for and protects me. At the end of the day, whatever else may be true about who I am and what I am experiencing, I am first, foremost, and ever will be held fast within His household—He is with me.

Thus, because He is with me, I will not be made less. The very essence of my being remains in fullness. My identity, my worth, my real self is not rooted in what I have or what I lose in this life, but in my unending condition of being part of His house, continually shepherded by Him.

This reality holds true for the long haul of my life—the complete length of my days—for as long as I exist. My identity, the certainty of my hope for the present and the future, my true value as a person—these are anchored within my established place in relationship with the LORD, whose household is strong and whose ongoing interaction with His household members continually demonstrates His faithful work of tending to and caring for His people. He reveals His own identity by this involvement with us, even as He shares His identity with us in the process.

Such understanding often requires a great deal of trust. This can be a real challenge for humans who live in a fallen world in which trust is frequently rewarded with violation. We learn very early that it could be quite unwise to be vulnerable to a person who is powerful. Unfortunately, we tend to view the LORD as a giant, fallen human as well, and find ourselves struggling to expect the LORD to be anything other than our past experiences with imperfect people.

This psalm calls for a change of view. I may not understand why some things are happening in my life. I may not recognize the LORD's presence with me in an immediate situation. I may be deeply discouraged, angry, confused, frustrated, or afraid in the face of my current circumstances. These things, however, do not change the fundamental facts of the nature of who I am in relationship to the unchanging and faithful LORD.

In the big picture, in the full length of my days, these truths stand—I belong in the household of the LORD, the LORD is continuously tending to my needs, and because of these things, when all is said and done, I will not be reduced. I am fully secure through my relationship with Him.

Can this be true within the complex, challenging concerns of my very real experiences in this world? The psalmist begins and ends this psalm with the firmly stated images of the LORD's faithfulness in relationship to His people, but the picture does not stop there. These parallel images of the LORD as the One who is perpetually shepherding me, and the LORD as the One in whose family

I firmly belong, provide the frame in which the detailed picture will be further showcased.

The poetic form of the psalm continues to draw me deeper into the specific ways that the LORD tends to the needs of His people and secures our lives within His household. Rather than avoiding the aspects of this life that seem to challenge our belief in the LORD's faithfulness, the psalmist plunges in fearlessly to the very issues that might make us question the reality of the LORD's good presence.

This psalm is not an ode to a "sugar-coated" description of what life may involve. Rather, it is a celebration of what it is to live this life, for real, with all it brings, in the ongoing understanding that <u>life is good not because it is easy; life is good because He is with me!</u>

CHAPTER 2

Because You Are with Me
I AM ENRICHED

*In pastures of new grass He makes me stretch out
and lie down . . .
Surely goodness and steadfast love will pursue me
all the days of my life.*

As the poetry of Psalm 23 continues, the psalmist explores specific ways in which my life is enriched because the Lord is shepherding me and because I am established within His household—because He is with me.

This next partnership of ideas in the psalm unites a scene of the sheep peacefully grazing in a beautiful enclosed pasture of fresh green grass with the imagery of some of life's most desired treasures—goodness and deeply satisfying relationship. Together, these pictures show an experience of safety, rest, and rich provision of that which sustains life. What an incredible contrast to the normal chaos of the broken world in which we exist!

Just to look across a vibrant meadow, newly sprouted by the spring rains, brings a sense of peace and comfort to the soul. And the Shepherd wants to lead us to that kind of place in our life's journey, not just to arrive there, but to stretch out and lie down for a while. That is, I am to choose to rest in the provision of life-sustaining resources to which He leads me in this particular season.

Why is the essential act of lying down required? Why do I have to stay in this hedged in field, spacious though it may be, when there might be something better elsewhere? Shouldn't I be continually looking over the next hill, roaming and seeking the next "big thing"?

Every aspect of our market-driven, "success"-oriented, perpetually dissatisfied, compare-my-life-with-the-rich-and-famous culture tells us that is exactly what we should be doing. Especially when our own immediate assessment of the situation has determined that current "needs" outweigh the resources we see around us. But the psalmist says, "Follow your Shepherd to the meadow that will really feed your soul, stretch out, get comfortable and lie down!"

This is about priorities. This is about understanding where genuine abundant life may be found. This is first and last all about trust—

> Trust that this Shepherd is bringing me to the best supply of life-giving resource for this season of my life.
>
> Trust that this Shepherd will lead me to another meadow at the right time should I need such a change in diet for life-giving sustenance.

I Am Enriched

Trust that this Shepherd knows all about my vulnerabilities, as I stretch out and rest.

Trust that this Shepherd really understands what I need, more than I do.

Trust that feeding on the resources this Shepherd provides enables me to produce fruit that fulfills my purpose as His creation—the very essence of genuine success.

This kind of trust is much easier to discuss than to embrace. Among life's challenges, both the real ones and those we've inflated by our broken cultural norms, is such trust even possible? The poetic partnership created here by the psalmist encourages us to attempt it by giving an important insight into another aspect of the situation.

Whatever else I'm experiencing in my life, in the pastures where this Shepherd leads me, goodness and steadfast love are also in the picture. And not only are they present, but they are in hot pursuit of me.

Every day—

    with absolute certainty—

        because He is with me.

What are these things, this "goodness" and "steadfast love," that so persistently chase me? Consistently, in the Scriptures, goodness is a quality of God's own nature. God is good. Goodness is also inevitably associated with pleasantness and delight. There is joy in goodness.

Goodness is the condition of being fully who we are created to be, and the fulfillment of all that the Creator purposed in the creation. Goodness is the ability to function with complete freedom exactly as we are designed to function—the ultimate success!

Where there is goodness, all is right with the world created by God who is good. Goodness is a wonderful thing, and that is why, in the very depths of our being, we all crave it. Though tragically, in our fallen world, we often look for it in places where it will not be found.

As we do also with relational faithfulness, or "steadfast love." We are creatures of community—designed to live most fully in relationships with God and with each other. When we think back over our lives, are not the best and most precious moments those in which we experienced deep connections with other living beings? There, we knew that we were each fully committed to the good of the other and found ourselves in a place of rich fulfillment and perfect safety.

Do we not all long for genuine loyalty in this world, where we cannot survive alone? Do we not all struggle with deep fears that such steadfast love will not be found? Truly, such fears often keep us from risking personal commitments, and yet what greater treasure is there than a proven, trustworthy friend? Conversely, what greater damage is done to us and by us than that which is the result of broken loyalties? Goodness and relational faithfulness are lost there—and so are we.

Our very humanity depends on the elements of goodness and relational faithfulness. Our survival, both as individuals and as communities, must have no less as its core. We know this instinctively, yet we live in a fractured world. So we run and we endlessly pursue, but we do not find because we have not yet understood the reality of life with the LORD—life with the Shepherd who created us and knows exactly what we need in order to thrive as His creation.

I AM ENRICHED

The fact is, no matter what I think I see or know or need, and no matter what I'm experiencing in the present situation, either real or imagined, there is hope. Genuine goodness and relational faithfulness are always pursuing me because He who *is* the Good and Faithful One is with me. Ironically, I often don't realize this because I'm not looking, as I frantically run around in my own futile and exhausting pursuit of the very things which are trying to catch me as I run!

If, in the meadow to which the Shepherd has led me, these wonderful life-giving things are really chasing after me—and they are, even if I can't see them right now—then there is only one reasonable course of action:

Stop running!

It seems such a simple thing, yet we struggle to make this choice. Why are we so driven to run all the time?

We run because of fear.

We run because of stress.

We run because of pressure to perform.

We run because of failure.

We run because of disappointment.

We run because of lack of direction.

We run because of feeling overwhelmed.

Most of all, we run because everyone else seems to be running!

Into this ongoing chaos, the psalmist calls us to stop, remember who we really are, and take a good long look around. The LORD is shepherding me. I am complete and my identity and value are utterly secure in Him. I am part

Because You Are with Me

of His family for the entirety of my existence. He is leading me into safe places of rich provision for my soul. There is resource right in front of me and even more resources are actively chasing me every day of my life—no matter what I see, feel, think, assume, imagine or fear.

The only sensible choice is to dare to trust this Shepherd—to stop running, lie down, and take in what is provided for my sustenance here, in this place, in this moment.

> I wait for the next wave of goodness and faithfulness to catch me—
>
> because it will—
>
> because He is with me.

My task is not to chase after success. My success is to be who He has created me to be, fully trusting that He will be all that He is without fail. In this, I will feast upon His goodness and faithfulness in the safe green pasture of His presence. Feeding upon such richness, I am enabled anew as the good and faithful person He has made me to be. I am strong and ready for the next leg of the journey—because He is with me.

Chapter 3

Because You Are with Me
I AM REFRESHED

To waters of quiet rest He tenderly guides me . . .
My cup is filled to overflowing.

As the psalmist continues to explore the ways in which the Shepherd cares for His sheep, another image of His faithfulness is put forth for the reader's reflection.

The prior picture addressed our ongoing need to stop chasing after things that will not feed us. Instead, we trust in the LORD enough to stop running, to allow the goodness and faithfulness of His presence to "catch" us, and to take in the rich provision we so desperately need in this season in order to be who He has created us to be.

But the picture is not yet complete. Immediately following this essential truth is another aspect of the LORD's faithful provision for the ongoing lives of His people, for life with the Shepherd involves an ongoing journey. To help us understand its nature, and our experience of it, the psalmist uses the comparative idea of water.

Perhaps those who live in desert regions have the best opportunity to appreciate the full value of this element! Water is the most fundamental need for sustaining life. We simply cannot survive without it, and we must be continually renewed in it. We may store this vital resource in our bodies for a time, but we are designed to require continual refilling as the demands of our existence use up the supply. In other words,

> we have been intentionally created—
> to be perpetually in need.

This aspect of our undeniable dependence can be very disquieting! How we long to believe that we do not rely on anyone or anything else beyond ourselves! How much of our time and energy is devoted to that illusion of self-absorption! In our continuously "plugged-in" world in which we desperately seek affirmation of our significance every minute of every day, we often put forth photographic panoramas of ourselves that we hope will show everyone how together we are and how important we are—how *un*-needy we are.

Even within church culture, we urgently attempt to impress—to be the one who is always "blessed," and always pouring out into others, and always "the spiritual one." Then, one day, we wake up to discover that instead of really living life, our efforts to maintain this self-created persona have depleted every resource we have. We are utterly dried up and empty inside, having been taken unaware of the deep loneliness that has pervaded our true souls, which are hiding somewhere behind our social media postings and carefully constructed personal appearances.

How ironic that in our efforts to display that glowing image of complete self-sustained independence, we have only managed to exhaust the small store of resource we had, demonstrating even more how truly needy we are!

To make matters worse, at this point in the process we may notice others nearby with a splash of water left in their carefully hoarded, self-filled water bottles. Then, we try to meet our own thirst by grabbing their little bit of resource, ultimately using them up for ourselves, too. Things can get pretty intense in the desert, where water is scarce, and people are increasingly desperate!

Is there any hope? <u>Perhaps the first step is to recognize that our built-in, undeniable, and unavoidable ongoing need for personal resource is not a weakness to be denied or an enemy to be overcome. It is, instead, a recurring invitation to return to the real resource that renews life within us and to drink deeply.</u>

Fortunately, we have a Shepherd who knows where the water sources are found in this journey of life. And they do not provide just any old liquid that might do. On the contrary, these vibrant springs are described as places of true rest. That is, they are opportunities for me to be completely at ease because I know I belong and am safe. I am in the right place—a place designed to provide me with the exact resource I need in order to live and thrive in this part of the journey.

But I cannot find this oasis on my own. I am completely dependent on the Shepherd to get me there.

And He will get me there—

    because He is with me.

Because You Are with Me

This Shepherd doesn't just hand me a water bottle, give me a little shove and say, "See you on the other side, if you make it. Good luck out there!" This Shepherd makes sure I get to the source of the water I absolutely must have.

The psalmist's word choice here describes the way a shepherd personally escorts the sheep, especially the very vulnerable ones. Thus, the picture of this Shepherd is that of a true guide. He takes me by the hand, and we walk together to this place of essential resource for my life and well-being—this place that He knows is there, even when I do not. This Shepherd does not leave me behind.

Even if I'm slow.

Even if I'm weak or injured.

Even if I'm heavily weighed down.

Even if I'm just learning how to walk for the first time.

Even if He has to carry me.

<u>This Shepherd will get me to the water. My job is to recognize that He is with me</u>, trusting that He knows where the good water is better than I do, especially when I'm very thirsty and can't see the oasis yet.

This doesn't mean I must pretend I'm not thirsty or try to convince myself and others that I don't really need water to live. Not at all! If I've somehow convinced myself that I am beyond the need for refreshment, I could stand right in front of the most life-giving resource, refusing to acknowledge my need, while dying of thirst—as the Shepherd stands there with me longing for me to drink deeply of that which He has provided!

Nothing could be further from the psalmist's description of our journey on this thirsty path. The parallel imagery of the psalm shows that when we do get to these springs of life-giving sustenance to which He guides us, we don't just take a sip—we get saturated, while our cup overflows!

As the poetry of the psalm unfolds, the image of the place of oasis is joined with the picture of an unglazed clay jar filled with water until it spills out over the top and soaks into the jar itself. Thus, we are not only filled with this renewing resource, we are drenched in it to the point that its life-giving effects are not only found on the inside, but they also become clearly evident on the outside.

<u>Having once been so dry I would desperately grasp from others to attempt to save myself at their expense, I now have so much I cannot help but give freely from the excess. How can this be?</u>

It is my shell of a broken and spent life, my dry clay cup that now overflows, but it overflows because the LORD personally brings me from the place of emptiness to the place of abundance—from a parched reality to the reality of oasis, where great need meets great supply. Both are genuine, and I will experience both on this journey.

> I cannot drink deeply at the oasis if I am not willing to acknowledge my thirst.
>
> I cannot drink deeply at the oasis if I don't choose to drink.
>
> I cannot drink deeply at the oasis if I cannot find it.
>
> I cannot find the oasis by myself because I don't know where it is.

I am reminded once again that I am entirely dependent on the Shepherd to help me along the way. In the demands of the journey, I will again and again need renewed provision of life-giving resource.

Because You Are with Me

But that is all right—I have a Shepherd who continually leads me to the next stream, who knows just how far I can go on the last supply, and who is well acquainted with every safe and quiet place of rest along the way. This Shepherd can even create such oases where they did not exist before!

I can walk in confidence with this Guide, even if I am beginning to feel the inevitable pangs of thirst in my ongoing neediness. That need calls me again to His presence. I depend on Him and will continue this journey well supplied and repeatedly refreshed—because He is with me.

CHAPTER 4

Because You Are with Me
I AM WHOLE

He restores my soul . . .
You heal my head with oil.

The beautiful pastoral scenes at the beginning of Psalm 23 create a picture of peace, rest, provision, and safety. However, they are also placed within the larger circumstance of a journey—the ongoing experience of life in a real world. An early hint that there may be trouble in that process is given in the simple statement, "He restores my soul."

On the one hand, this declaration gives great hope—the promise of restoration. On the other hand, such hope implies a prior condition that is not so pleasant. Why would my soul need restoration if it has not already been lost in some way?

Perhaps we have lost our souls in the all-consuming pursuit of success in this world, where everything else is sacrificed to the insatiable acquisition of money, fame, or the ultimate goal—absolute power over other people. Even as we gain more and more of these things, we often experience increasing emptiness or become numb inside.

Perhaps our souls have been taken from us when we got in the way of someone else who was in pursuit of such things. This could happen in a single, life-shattering event, or slowly, daily being used up and utterly spent by a ruthless corporation, an unhealthy relationship, or even a church community that has lost sight of the true teachings of Christ in its heedless pursuit of worldly "success."

Perhaps we have lost our souls in the process of just surviving the rigors of existing in a broken world for which we were not actually created and equipped. Chronic illness, loss of loved ones, the suffering of our children, the indignities of poverty, rampant injustice and violation—the overwhelming mass of troubles in this fallen existence in which we are caught up and seem to have inadequate ability to bring substantive change or even to understand. They wear on our souls. They erode life itself.

Into these places of hopelessness and despair in the brokenness of our very real world, the psalmist calmly declares, "He restores my soul." He gives me my life back.

In a world that continually takes life from me,
the Shepherd returns life to me.

This idea of human life, or the "soul," is holistic and all-compassing. That is, my soul is everything that makes me distinctively who I am as He created me to be—my true self. And while all the forces of evil and decay that infuse this fallen world are actively at work to destroy that creation, the LORD is at work to return me to that wondrously created person He originally designed.

The restored soul is full of life and human dignity, displaying the image of God in beauty, strength, and wholeness—uniquely gifted and divinely empowered to walk in confidence and authority. Each restored soul is an essential part of the LORD's ongoing, redemptive, life-giving work within this fractured world so filled with lost souls.

How may such an outcome be achieved, especially when my immediate circumstances may seem unchanged in the devastating impact of their current broken reality? In the poetry of this psalm, the parallel thought here brings further insight into how my soul may be restored and the life of my true self returned. The psalmist states that the LORD has "anointed my head with oil."

In the world of the Hebrew Bible, the act of applying oil to someone usually emphasizes one of two ideas—to commission someone for specific purpose in service, or to bring someone to improved health and well-being. Here, the psalmist has chosen specific language to highlight the second option of improved health and well-being. The "anointing" described here is an act of healing—literally, to "fatten up" someone in need—to bring someone from weakness to strength.

The idea is further emphasized with the picture of rich, fatty olive oil as part of this anointing by the Shepherd. Such oil restores nutrients, while soothing and softening the chafed and hardened places that have been subjected to the harsh elements of nature.

While the anointing of a person's head with oil would not be uncommon in this culture, as well as applying oil to other parts of the body exposed to wind and sun, it does not seem to be coincidental that the psalmist emphasizes the healing of a person's head in parallel with the idea of restoring the soul.

In ancient times, these very practical people associated a person's head with life itself, as everything we need to maintain life—water, food, and air to breathe—enters our bodies through our heads. Of course, our brain function and thinking ability are also essential to our ability to survive and thrive.

Thus, to bring health and wholeness to a person's head not only brings comfort and restores life there, but also restores the ability of that person to receive every other aspect of life-giving resource, such as the food and water that have already been symbolically described in the prior verses of the psalm.

In other words, this Shepherd not only heals part of the person's wounds in the current moment, but in doing so also improves the person's ability to receive restoration, so that even greater healing might continue to flow throughout the entire person over time—He heals my ability to receive ongoing healing!

How does the LORD do this? He pours out abundant, rich, soothing, healing resource into the very places of my being through which I take in everything that I need as His creation to be all that He has created me to be. And this generous outpouring of life-giving restoration comes because He is with me.

In those places where my experiences have caused me to become calloused and hard, His presence softens, restoring sensitivity and responsiveness.

In those places where my thinking has become chafed and cynical with the irritating hot and sandy winds of brokenness in a self-absorbed society, His presence

I Am Whole

soothes and renews hope in what He can do beyond our failures.

In those places where the losses I've experienced have broken my will to continue living, His presence fills in empty places and becomes one with my pain, easing the depth of its sting and promoting opportunity for regeneration of new life in days to come.

In those places where my ability to receive life-giving resource I desperately need has been damaged by my own mistreatment of myself, or by the mistreatment of others toward me, His presence brings the very nutrients I need to recover and to return to my original purpose as one who is created in His image of holiness and beauty.

And with every encounter of His presence that brings completed healing to my ability to receive life from Him, the full reality of my being as He has created me to be is further returned to me.

My soul, my true self—

> all that makes me who I am and forever will be—

> is being returned to me,

>> because He is with me!

The truth of this reality is the very heart of the Gospel. The Shepherd knows what it is to live with the full effects of this broken world. He knows what it is to experience the loss of loved ones. He knows what it is to be buffeted by the hot wind of adversity. He gives and gives, only to be dishonored by the recipients of His generosity. He became the very reality of battered and bruised humanity. He experienced the slow and certain personal loss, as life drained from His physical body.

He also experienced the restoration of life. He who has walked the path of human death has both founded and walked the path of human resurrection. This is my Shepherd, and He pours out healing upon me today that I might be strengthened to take in all that sustains my soul, today and for all the days to come.

Whatever this journey through life in a fallen world requires, and even if its rigors take from me parts of the very essence of my being, hope yet remains. As I journey on with my Shepherd, my Healer, the losses of my soul can only give way to its restoration—because He is with me.

CHAPTER 5

Because You Are with Me
I AM CONFIDENT

He leads me in paths of rightness because of His name . . .
You set before me a table facing my enemies.

The opening verses of Psalm 23 have described an ongoing journey with the Shepherd, who provides places of rest, refreshing, and healing. He carefully tends to the needs of the sheep and helps them along the way. At this point, the psalmist highlights again the guidance of the Shepherd. This time, He is described as One who leads the sheep by actively showing them the right way.

In other words, in addition to being present with the sheep as they go along together, this Shepherd personally goes first to face whatever lies ahead—the very essence of genuine leadership. Consequently, the Shepherd does not require anything of the sheep that He, Himself, has not already experienced. Indeed, the Shepherd knows these paths very well.

The imagery is further strengthened by the psalmist's wording. This path is not some random way to go. This is literally a worn rut. These trails have been formed and hardened by being traveled over again and again. They may cross all kinds of terrain and be very narrow in places—even following ledges near dangerous precipices—but the trails themselves are sound. Many have followed them and have safely reached their destination.

In fact, every time the Shepherd brings yet another sheep along the way, their shared footsteps further develop the worn ruts that will serve to help others follow them successfully in the future, as the Shepherd leads each one along the paths He knows so well. And every time the LORD guides another one of His people along, He goes first, experiencing each specific path with each one of us anew—every time, because He is with us.

The paths themselves have purpose—they are paths of rightness. How many times have we struggled to determine what is right? As our lives become increasingly complicated, this question becomes more intimidating.

From a biblical perspective, rightness includes that which is ethical and just, rich in generosity, and promoting relational wholeness. Rightness is evident when we truly reflect the nature of our Creator in the way we live and relate to each other and to the rest of creation.

Like goodness, rightness may be seen in the creation before the fall of humanity, when everything was just as the Creator designed it to be. Rightness promotes goodness and provides the level foundation for its effectiveness.

No wonder the LORD is so familiar with these rightly rutted paths! Who better to lead in the right way than the One who established rightness in the first place? Of course, He knows every turn in the road, every wide and narrow place, every lovely view and difficult terrain. And most importantly, when He leads in rightness,

> He shows the way personally—
>> both in action and in being—
>>> because He is with us.

How comforting to know that I do not have to have all the answers. Even if I cannot figure out what "right" looks like in my immediate circumstance, while I am on the particular path in which He leads me, I don't always have to understand it—I can rely on the Guide who does.

And the better I come to know the Guide, the more readily I will recognize the paths He has created by His own constancy of character and conduct over the experience of the whole journey—because He continually shows me the way of rightness by going first.

Clearly, the LORD's own reputation is part of the process. The psalmist affirms that the LORD leads us along these paths because of His name—because of who He is and who He is becoming known to be, as He guides people through life in the real world and its maze of circumstances.

Because we are part of His household, we share in His identity and honor. To follow this Shepherd is to become like Him—to be consistently untwisted from our fallen, distorted, and broken ways and to be restored to rightness—to the original design of human dignity that reflects His nature.

Whatever else may be happening to me and all around me on this journey, I can be confident that the paths of rightness in which He leads me will ultimately result in my full redemption as His creation.

And I will arrive there safely—

because He is with me.

Every sheep may not take the exact same path—each life has its own distinct purpose as given by the Creator. Yet each one who follows this Shepherd will be guided to rightness by the One who *is* Right. His very nature ensures that those who truly follow Him will be made right along the way, as we continue to walk with Him.

But this journey does not occur in a vacuum. We live and relate and make choices in a broken world that is all too real. Even the path of redemption winds its way through that reality, and the journey to wholeness does not happen overnight.

The parallel imagery in the psalm indicates that enemies will come my way, even as I journey on the right path! The comparison of the two themes in the psalm helps to identify these hostile forces. They aren't my enemies simply because they don't like me. They are my enemies because they oppose the rightness that is defined and demonstrated by the character and example of the Shepherd I follow.

If we consider the ongoing description of the Shepherd in this psalm, specific details about these enemies of His rightness become clear—

They reduce human dignity.

They seek to separate us from relationship with the LORD and each other.

They convince us to pursue and trust false images of self-sufficiency and success.

They motivate us to use and violate others out of our own insecurities.

They plunder the soul and resist restoration.

These opponents, perpetuated in our broken humanity, bring very real hostility into our world. And, so, they also become part of our journey—sometimes through the choices of others and sometimes through our own folly. Of course, we also have a very real enemy in the spirit realm who epitomizes such evils.

What is the response of the Shepherd to these deeply distressing forces of oppression threatening the sheep? He sets up a picnic at the side of the road! The stark contrast of these images is so startling that we may not fully grasp its significance. What is happening here?

In ancient times, preparing a shared meal could have significant meaning, especially since food supplies were highly valued and protected. Sharing food was a tangible expression of showing honor to another person and of confirming relational commitments. The picture of the LORD setting a table before me facing my enemies provides a strong statement of my connection to Him. He might as well hold up a sign saying, "Come near this one and you'll have to deal with Me, too!"

This Shepherd openly confronts that which is hostile to rightness, even as He leads in rightness. And a leader requires a follower. This confrontation is a shared meal—I face these enemies right alongside the Shepherd with confidence. We are in this together, even when the opposer of rightness is my own brokenness!

My brokenness as an individual and our brokenness together as fallen humanity does not intimidate this Shepherd, and so it does not have to intimidate me—because He is with me.

He is leading me in rightness—showing me the way.

I do not face my enemies alone.

There is definite irony here. Usually, the enemies are predators who devour sheep. Here, however, the sheep get to eat the dinner, rather than becoming the main course themselves! The language here indicates that the LORD is making a spectacle of this meal. It is a prominent display, declaring His strong alliance with His people, especially when our journey on the right path is threatened.

Because this Shepherd is with me, He shows me the way forward, providing what I need every step of the way, ensuring ultimate victory in my life, as I become more and more like the One I'm following, while I walk with Him—

Even when I face opposition.

Even when I am my own greatest enemy.

Even when the journey becomes very dark, indeed.

CHAPTER 6

Because You Are with Me
I AM COURAGEOUS

*Even if I walk in the darkest valley,
I will not be afraid of harm . . .
Your rod and Your staff, they comfort me.*

As the psalmist approaches the central theme of the poem, the imagery intensifies to its starkest picture. Again, the poet does not hesitate to embrace the reality of life's unavoidable challenges, while yet continuing to celebrate the benefits of the Shepherd's presence in our lives.

Here, the picture of a valley in deepest darkness is given, not just a shadow or shaded place. In desert regions, shade is often described positively, as protection from the hot sun. Instead, here the psalmist describes a valley as dark as death itself—a potentially hazardous place of the complete unknown.

Those places beyond prior experience and our ability to navigate or understand.

Those places fraught with imaginings of the worst that can possibly occur.

Those places where we have no control over what is happening or its outcomes.

Those places where we cannot see even the next step right in front of us—not knowing if it will bring firm ground under our feet, or that last step off the cliff leading to utter destruction of all we hold dear.

Those places where we don't just feel like or imagine we cannot go on, but we really cannot go on as we have been—it is truly the end of some significant part of ourselves.

Those places that no matter how hard we tried to avoid them, or prepared to outsmart them, or empowered ourselves to overcome them, we have ended up here anyway, and we simply cannot fix this.

In short, those places bringing the deep responses of indescribable and debilitating sorrow, disorientation, isolation, and, ultimately, fear—fear that makes us want to run frantically or to remain stunned and immovably frozen on the spot where we stand.

Perhaps the most distressing aspect of this psalm is the calm assumption by the psalmist that such valleys of utter darkness are probably going to be part of our real-life experience in this journey through a broken world.

Maybe I am here because of someone else.

Maybe I am here because of my own choices.

Maybe I am here because it looked like a nice little valley from the outside, but it ended up enclosing around me in life-threatening ways I never imagined possible.

Maybe I am here because the only way forward is through this valley.

Maybe I am here because the LORD led me here for reasons He may or may not be telling me.

Whatever has brought me into this dark place, what do I do now? Here the psalmist makes an unexpected declaration. While fear may be the most reasonable reaction to such a situation, that is exactly what the psalmist says we will not do. In this place of complete darkness, with no answers and no sense of direction and no means to achieve a positive outcome or to change my circumstances, I will not be afraid of harm.

How is this kind of courage remotely possible?

Because the LORD is with me.

We must recognize that the psalmist does not deny the possibility of harm, but rather its power to dominate us with fear. Such freedom comes with the understanding that we are not alone—the Shepherd is with us, even when darkness is all we can see in this moment. And this Shepherd comes well equipped!

In the parallel thought, the psalmist describes two specific elements further explaining why fear may not possess us within life's greatest difficulties—the Shepherd's rod and staff. Both tools have similar multipurpose usage. They are designed to serve as weapons against predators who seek to destroy. They are an extension of the Shepherd's arm to ensure the sheep's well-being by maintaining closeness to the Shepherd. The Shepherd gathers the sheep, making sure none are left behind, entangled, or lost—great comforts in the darkest places!

The psalmist's picture, then, becomes complete. What do we fear most when we are in utter darkness in our lives?

> The predator we cannot see who seeks our destruction—both the imagined and the real.
>
> Our potential to make a wrong step toward an even more dangerous situation, especially when we cannot see our way or have made wrong steps before.
>
> The inability to free ourselves from the complex entanglements that make us more vulnerable to those who seek our destruction, especially if we've experienced prior trauma.
>
> Or perhaps the greatest fear—that we will be abandoned and alone in this dark place—without deliverance and without hope for a future that goes beyond the valley of our present circumstance.
>
> But there is relief from such fear—
>
> > because we are not alone—
> >
> > > because He is with us.
>
> Because He is with us, we have a Shepherd who is ever mindful of our situation and who never leaves us behind. He continually extends His hand to gather us close.
>
> Because He is with us, we have a Shepherd who persistently seeks out the one who is lost or stuck and who makes the way in the darkness for safe return.

Because He is with us, though the predator may attempt to destroy, the Shepherd is armed and vigilant, and He is ultimately greater than all.

Because He is with us, though we cannot see right now and do not understand what is happening around us, we can know with certainty that this Shepherd will personally guide and even carry His sheep through the deepest darkness to the other side of this valley, as the journey together goes on.

And because we have experienced His presence in the very heart of such fearsome difficulties, we know Him now in ways we did not before—though we may not yet recognize or appreciate this fact as we wait in the dark. The psalmist recognizes the connection between our experiences of dark valleys and the changes they can make in our relationship with the LORD.

It is no coincidence that a shift in language occurs here, at the very center of the psalm. Right here, the psalmist moves from referring to the LORD in general third-person language, "He" and "His," to the more intimate second-person language, "You" and "Your."

That is, here, in the blackest and deepest darkness, in the deadly shadows of the greatest difficulties of our lives, an understanding of His presence and its vital role in our very existence brings us from a place of knowing about His qualities as a Person to knowing Him even more personally.

Through the dark valley, my perspective intensifies from a descriptive recognition of "this is who the LORD is in matters concerning me" to the more intimate conversation with Him, "This is who You are to me."

Even in this dark place.

Because You Are with Me

Especially in this dark place.

Ever after this dark place.

Because You are with me in the most desperate times of my life, when I cannot feel Your presence, being numb to cope with the present pain, there is hope.

Though I may be surrounded by darkness right now, its accompanying fear does not rule me. The LORD and I continue the journey together. I can keep walking because He will not lose me. This present valley of the darkest shadow in which I may now find myself will end—we will go through together. I am never alone.

> The LORD guides me amid darkness,
>
> > leading me through the darkness to the light,
>
> > > because He is with me.

This psalm tells me a profound truth of this journey with the LORD. The valley of deadly darkness is a place where two realities confront each other—the very real situation in my life and His very real presence in my life. In this dramatic encounter, the certainties described throughout the psalm also meet, so that I might understand vital truths in dark places—

I do not belong to the darkness, but to the Shepherd.

The darkness does not determine my identity, the Shepherd does.

The darkness does not hold me, His goodness and faithfulness do.

The darkness does not direct my path, the Shepherd does.

The darkness will end, but the Shepherd will not.

I Am Courageous

I do not have to live in fear of the darkness within this world's realm. The darkness does not have the last word—the valley is never the end of the story. Whatever this life brings, when all is said and done,

> We journey on together,
>> I know my Shepherd well,
>>> and I am being made whole,
>>>> because He is with me.

EPILOGUE

The LORD is the foundation of my identity and worth.
His presence is goodness and faithfulness pursuing me.

    The LORD is the sustenance feeding my soul.
    His presence is my shelter of rest.

The LORD is the resource renewing my strength.
His presence is my place of contentment.

    The LORD is the source of my healing.
    His presence is my restoration from loss.

The LORD is rightness, leading me to wholeness.
His presence is my protection against destruction.

The LORD is my future, even amid uncertainty.
His presence is my deliverance from fear's grasp.

    You, O LORD, are my Shepherd.
    I have hope today, tomorrow, and always,
    Because I know You—
    Because You are with me!

Made in the USA
Coppell, TX
11 November 2020

41149312R10033